The Heart of The
Bitter Almond Hedge Sutra

Thanissara

SACRED MOUNTAIN PRESS

www.dharmagiri.org

Copyright © 2013 Thanissara

All rights reserved.

ISBN: 1490567305

ISBN 13: 9781490567303

Library of Congress Control Number: 2013911933
CreateSpace Independent Publishing Platform
North Charleston, South Carolina

In Honour of

Madiba

Cowards die many times before their death;
The valiant never taste death but once.
Of all the wonders I have yet heard
It seems to me most strange that people should fear,
Seeing that death, a necessary end,
Will come when it will come. *

*While imprisoned on Robben Island, an inmate took the works of Shakespeare to the political prisoners on Cell Block C and asked them to mark their favourite passages. Madiba (Mr Nelson Mandela) did not hesitate. He turned to Julius Caesar, act 2, scene 2, and circled this passage.

Introduction

In the Tibetan Buddhist tradition, Dharma teachings are sometimes hidden in a distilled form and left in a sacred place to be revealed at a later age. When a learned guru, or *terton,* finally discovers and deciphers them, they open into a hologram of transmission and understanding. These teachings are called *terma.*

In humbler ways, poetry has a similar function. It tries to capture lived experiences and insights, while exposing the reader to a flash of connection and understanding through a few lines or even just a word or two. The task of the poet is to mirror life, to extract meaning from the flow of events, and to challenge, shock, or affirm what often eludes articulation. In doing so, the poet hopes to imprint the mind of another in such a way that evokes and urges a deeper engagement with the experiences communicated. A poet also aims to relieve his or her own soul of impossible burdens through the process of expression or, on the contrary, to reveal awakenings, or perhaps through a simple brush stroke, to portray the essence and mystery of "what is." The poet wants to share, describe, disturb, and sometimes soothe and inspire, while uncovering what gets missed when only the surface is skimmed. In short, the poet hopes to transmit haunting and evocative truths by combining distilled and contrasting perceptions and succinct imagery which hold power.

One of the most famous Buddhist *termas,* rendered in poetic fashion, is the Heart Sutra. The Heart Sutra is a pithy teaching which the Buddha is said to have taught, to those who could hear it, at Vulture Peak in Bihar, India, towards the end of his life. Scholars also say that it is a text emergent from within the mists of time, after the Buddha's demise, which challenged the hierarchal and priestly orthodoxy that Buddhism became. It does so by completely demolishing all methods, all accepted and conventional Buddhist teaching, all time-bound rituals, and all religiosities. It even takes away coveted attainments and all hard-earned knowledge. In short, it removes the currency of conceptual brilliance as a means to enlightenment. Instead, the sutra radically points the disciple (our clever and brilliant mind)—in this instance Shariputra, who represents the pinnacle of Buddhist "learnt" wisdom—back to the immediate and simple recognition of the seat of the sacred. This is the "deathless mind," which "knows directly." It is the empty, full, aware, present, listening, primordial, and intuitively wise heart, which is less concerned with objectifying the world as something to be known, controlled, or owned, and more focused on "coursing the depths" of the mystery, where the world and its "objects" dissolve into profound subjectivity. It is here that the intimacy of all things is revealed.

In sharp contradiction to the underlying nondual and seamless world of the Heart Sutra, the compulsive and addictive conceptual mind is susceptible to mapping out differences in ways that can swiftly degenerate into strife and conflict. Almost nowhere is this "setting apart" more pronounced than in colonialism, and in particular within the southernmost part of that great land mass of Africa, where it ultimately spawned the bitter fruit of apartheid. And it is here that this poem begins. The poem continues this theme by weaving the imperative of the Heart Sutra "to live without walls of the mind" into the contrasting impact of one of the most entrenched walls in history: that of extreme racist legislation, which has shaped South African society for over fifty years. Before that, three hundred years of colonial rule, which laid the ground for apartheid, wrought genocide on the First Nation People of the /Xam, San, Khoisan - the "Bushmen" tribes. Throughout the poem we hear their haunting voice. The Bushmen, our ancestors, lived thousands of years in symbiotic relationship with the forces of nature. The message of First Nation people is a sobering one. As we now spin farther and farther off track towards ecocide, they warn us of the urgency to honour the Earth before it's too late.

It's easy to pinpoint the particular madness of South Africa's brutal racial experiment and obsessive categorization of every citizen according to race and colour, but we don't have to look too far to recognize resonances of various forms of apartheid which prejudice against class, caste, gender, religious, and sexual orientation within all societies and countries. Even closer to home, our own minds are susceptible to conditioning that discriminates against the "other" due to "difference." But the ultimate apartheid is the mind's own division against the heart. This heart, which is deeper and more aware, and which intuitively knows the "intimacy of all things" is constantly pulled into the tyranny of the proliferating mind that tends to generate a fractured and incoherent world.

The inception and first demarcation of apartheid began with the planting of the bitter almond hedge (*brabejum stellatifolium*) by the pioneer governor Jan van Riebeeck, in about 1666. It was one of his first acts on arrival at the nascent colony of Cape Town. The intention was to create a boundary and isolate the white settlers from the KoiSan, the so-called Hottentots, and Africans whom, nevertheless, they needed to trade with. The remnant of this hedge can still be seen to this day in the beautiful Kirstenbosch National Botanical Garden, which adorns the side of Cape Town's iconic Table Mountain. The hedge became the first symbol of the laager, (circled wagons to ward off the enemy), and the later gated communities that define large areas of South Africa's contemporary cities, particularly in Johannesburg.

This outward sign of division inevitably becomes internalized, thereby laying the ground for irresolvable complex and contradictory emotions, the perceptual dissonance, illogical rationale, imbedded denial, and betrayals of the heart that apartheid birthed. Like any dysfunctional and abusive system that is perpetuated as the "norm," there has to be an internal split away from one's innate ethic and sensitivity to accommodate the pressure to conform. The price of abandoning a deeper empathy with one another is high. We end up perpetuating violence towards self, which is felt as a great inner pain that we seek to "medicate" through our addictions and distractions. Or, generated by divisive thinking, we perpetrate violence externally, even to the ultimate absurdity of war. At the end of the day, the sheer pressure of a socially conditioning collective isolated from the larger world, as was the case during the apartheid era, generated susceptibility towards defence against one's own deeper heart; a heart that in reality doesn't experience the world, or others, as apart from itself.

It is this fundamental separation from the heart's sensitive resonance with life, which is actually our common lot in an increasingly fractured world, that generates escalating spheres of disconnect and madness. The ultimate madness is the current drive for pathological power and obscene profit which is killing the ecological systems that our collective lives depend on. Apartheid has now morphed into our profound dissonance and divorce from Earth and nature. We have become arrogant, as if all of Mother Nature and her species, right down to the last patented seed and cell, are there to be owned and exploited for corporate and personal gain. Our collective state of complete and utter disrespect for the Earth, its species, and its limited resources, coupled with the political denial and corporate hijacking and distortion of true human values, has desecrated the sacred and rendered us soulless.

At this moment in our long evolutionary history, we are on the cusp of a "state shift" due to climate change, where there is no going back. From that point on, we are in freefall with the likelihood of massive ecocide, species extinction, and most likely an inability to sustain human life within an increasingly hostile environmental context. We may have already passed the point of no return, though there is some hope we may have a blink of an eye, in earth time, to turn our suicidal trajectory around. So on the cusp of losing everything; we really have only one choice. It is imperative to evolve out of our pathological, dualistic consciousness by living our profound interconnectedness as fully as we can. We are being called to make a radical shift and "be the change we want to live" in every moment, and in every way we possibly can. It is this new planetary reality, which shocks us awake, that is woven into the poem which, towards the end, moves into more hopeful territories of redemption.

At its core, the Heart Sutra imparts courage. This is the courage of the unfettered, free, and alive heart inherent within the deepest seat of inner listening. This is the heart that knows intuitively the "intimacy of all things." This heart is our birthright, a gift from the divine. This gift of divinity is not from some disembodied sky god who deigns to portion judgment and perhaps hand out a few crumbs if we're good, but it is a divinity imminent within ourselves, within all matter and all of creation. It exists within the sacredness of the Earth and within each living thing, each breath, our bodies, our sexuality, our relationships, our work, and all manifestation. It is the reclamation of this sacredness that is our task. In its iconic line *"Form is emptiness, emptiness is form,"* the sutra inducts us into the deepest mystery of consciousness and matter. In reality they are not separate. There is no objective world without the subject. Who that "subject" is, is the ultimate mystery. A mere glimpse of that adamantine "I Am That" burns up aeons of ignorance, and in an instant we are delivered into peace and courage. From there, although despair and fear touch the heart, and although stress and aversion, agitation, and sorrow visit as guests, the heart maintains its core integrity and unshakeable constancy.

And so the sutra encourages a leap, a radical shift. We are to *"relinquish all that is false, all dream thinking, and leap beyond the walls of the mind."* We are instructed to place our trust in the heart that is listening, aware, undivided, and waiting for our return. It is this heart that will save us. And it is this heart that maintains our humaneness, as we mediate between the reality of "no walls of the mind," and the negotiation of respectful and appropriate boundaries. To "live without walls of the mind" doesn't mean we don't recognize differences or that we can't be firm and set up healthy psychological boundaries when needed. It simply means that when we connect with the depth of awareness, we are then truly human, sensitive, ethical, and responsive. We haven't morphed into an unreflective, disembodied, fractured, addicted, and crazed machine that compensates the desperate ache of its inner void through endless consumption. And so it is to the human that the poem eventually appeals. Please maintain your humaneness; love it and care for it, and you will then know how to act in this crazed world.

Much of what is "crazed" is inherited from the unhealed generational wounds of the past. Contemporary neuropsychology tells us that when trauma is re-contextualised into acknowledged narrative, it literally alters the chemistry of the brain so that the resultant pathologies of traumatic events are less likely to pass onto the next generation. Intensifying the wounds of South Africa are the lost, unheard, and distorted stories of those who have been displaced. Historically the non-white population has endured dreadful sufferings which the white populations were mostly exempt, sufferings like genocide, the extreme excesses of forced removal, and feudalistic and migrant labour systems that kept people away from home, land, and family for years on end. Even so, the wars and trials of Southern Africa impacted white settlers in devastating ways that are not always clearly acknowledged. The poem touches into these themes of the generational struggle to survive, the grief of loss and separation, and its haunting residue of violence, addiction, abuse, and communal and family breakdown. It touches into the wreckage of the AIDS pandemic, one appalling symptom of the breakdown of community resilience, which has sent millions to an early death and which continues its devastating toll.

Yet regardless of race and colour, all have suffered some level of generational displacement through war, exile, and emigration as the forging of South Africa's complex history shaped, and continues to shape, the lives of everyone who has lived here. These days many elderly white parents see their children and grandchildren scattered across the globe as they search for stability and safety, leaving behind stories of murder and rape. And so this poem touches upon the human dilemma of ubiquitous lost roots which plays out within the regal landscape of Africa's beautiful land. As the karma of colonialism ripples through the generations and across continents, it also shapes the lands of the America's where similar roots of displacement, slavery and conquering birthed disturbing wars, social fractures and wonton desecration of the earth. Hopefully the poem makes clear that there's been enough suffering in these lands burnt through by conflict and dislocation. There has been enough suffering across our great earth for us all to wake up and say "STOP!" Acknowledging our stories, hearing the pain and suffering, helps us redeem our humanity. It is here we can rejoice in the great achievements of the human spirit that weather and overcome the many challenges placed before us.

At the end of the day, a poet doesn't know where their poem will go. They just make a mark on the page and then follow the inner prompting of what wants to be expressed. It is like a walk through a strange forest, where, at each turn, a new plant or tree is discovered and admired, or perhaps a strange creature appears and we are startled into a heightened wakefulness. This poem meanders through difficult and redemptive pathways, but it does so while also introducing the reader to South Africa's stunning and majestic landscapes and its dramatic weather patterns. When walked on, it is a landscape that opens into the greatness of the Earth's most generous bounty. But like any journey, it is enhanced and made worthwhile when taken with others. So I invite you to walk this journey with me as I share my love of the Heart Sutra and its subtle support through my twenty years of living within the residue of South Africa's wounds, challenges, wildness, beauty, and its ability to demonstrate that it can move back from the edge of self-destruction to inspire a hopeful new dawn once again.

Thanissara
November 2013

Dharmagiri, KwaZulu Natal, South Africa

Foreword

"The Heart of the Bitter Almond Hedge Sutra" is a profound guided meditation within a monumental poem. Our journey starts with a dedication to Nelson Mandela and his ability to inspire the human heart with the faith and courage needed for a journey into challenge. Even so, the poem always affirms our human ability to awaken to wisdom and joy in the midst of suffering and oppression, both in our own lives and in relation to the world. Modelled on the template of the Buddha's Four Noble Truths, the poem shows us harsh realities as the poet, Thanissara, names the causes of suffering, shows us states of suffering, but also shows us the cure and ways to practice to free ourselves from unnecessary suffering. Here we find the story of the human heart and how it becomes divided by fear and hate, yet what is also revealed is the way to access the *"heart which patiently waits"* so we can learn that *"every precious breath redeems your lost soul."*

The poem takes us on journey in which the magnificent continent of Africa becomes a symbol for life itself. *"In the times before we arrived/ lions stalk slowly/ their hot breath alive/ with the essence of stars."* Thanissara poignantly draws vivid portraits of people, animals and landscapes which she stretches to the universal. Mythic time becomes the frame for historical time as she captures the harsh realities of colonial Africa. Then in a finger snap we are spun across the world to feel the distress that pervades our world today as the planet is steadily plundered of its natural resources. Moving through different dimensions we are invited to practice with our own suffering and with the suffering of the world as we are asked to *"sit patiently through the night, and gather your wayward mind."* As we enter training in mindfulness, the presence of the poet is encouraging, supportive and continuous as we take in important lessons that have the potential to change our whole orientation within life.

The poem's penetrating cultural and psychological juxtapositions are grounded in a defining event from South Africa's history: the planting, in

1666, of a bitter-almond hedge that colonists grew as a barrier between their settlement and the rest of the African continent—a living wall that signals the arrival of the full force of colonialism which later birthed the stunted child of Apartheid; a stunting which eventually cut off the indigenous people from the grazing lands on which their sustenance depended. From this dense, tangled hedge grew the divisions of apartheid that came to shape every aspect of life in South Africa. The poet's wrenching portrait of the continent, punctuated throughout by the voices of Bushmen, has an intensity reflecting the more than twenty years that she and Kittisaro, her husband, spent teaching Buddhist meditation and the Dharma while also aiding South Africans devastated by poverty and AIDS.

The poem captures this exact time in history while also scoping in the daily barrage of bad news for the planet. We see vicious exploitation engineered in the great effort to maintain the economic profit of our capitalist system. "The Heart Sutra of the Bitter Almond Hedge" addresses the larger scale problem of the ecology of the earth: our dependence on oil, factory farming, and the resulting expropriation of land and extinction of species. The heartbreak and the fury we read between the lines impart a visceral understanding of our contemporary calamity, easily verified by a look at the Science Section of any reliable news source. The hedge, we soon see, is also emblematic of the human heart, which creates brutal divisions in the world because of the split inside itself: *The hedge's circle of thorns/ upholds distance/ from our muted heart.*

Here lie the ultimate causes of pain and war. This already broken heart, so eager to keep itself safe, cowers in its loneliness, keeping its ability to be one with "the other" at bay. We see the injured heart in its battered form, devoid of humanity, destructive, beset by lines, broken into fragments. We see the geometry of the heart in states of psychological trauma as the heart abandoned, abandoning, hurt, muted, faint, fallen down, lost, beaten down and cut-through, battered, broken into fragments, and devoid of humanity. The injured heart has a force that expresses its distress in the art of destruction.

Even as we enter the depth of the shadowed night of the heart, new ways call us on. Stay with it because the poem's cosmological sweep will carry you forward with its rhythmic momentum, its vivid images and the haunting beauty of the words themselves. After being led through a scorched landscape, you will be invited to a larger awareness that points the way from universal pain to our personal capacity for joy and wisdom. For those who enter a training of the mind, a radiant hope of the awakening of heart is affirmed in the progression of insights attainable through meditative practice which Thanissara has practiced and taught on three continents much of her adult life. She leads us in breathing through our deepest fears and aversions. As a reader one feels held, encouraged, and trained in wise response in the face of raw truths.

The deeper intent of the poem is to induct us into a beautiful litany of the awakening journey through the process of truth seeing and contemplation. This leads to the merciful, compassionate and wise heart which positively impacts the world. At every stage, the Buddhist Heart Sutra whispers in the background, urging us to open our hearts to the "intuitive intelligence" of our capacity for love. Rather than losing our power, *"Do not wander that twilight alone,"* we are invited to *"Really love your life, your Earth/ your all other living beings"*—that is, to live in Enlightenment, which is *"to be intimate with all things."* By learning how to embody this oneness, we gain the power to *"Hold together"* and *"not spiral down,"* awakening instead to *"the wild, shamanic power/ of the heart's peace pulse."* Embedded in this arc of understanding is a call to action, urging each of us to shatter, in our own way, the walls that imprison us and the rest of humanity. It is no coincidence that the poem is dedicated to Nelson Mandela, a fitting model for the bravery such engagement demands.

Right from the start of the poem, we are offered glimpses of human consciousness from the context of vastly different cultural conditions than our own, helping us see beyond our small selves. Throughout we hear the voices of Bushmen: *"A star is like our heart at the time in which we die, for it shoots..."* Ancient sensibilities may appear foreign to our modern minds as we may more comfortably recognize the thought *"I like...to have my ducks in a row."* as appears in our culture. But the impressions from a time-gone-by reflect into our current dilemma inviting us to have the humility to recognize that our empires have entailed the devastation of First Nation people, their cultures and their lands.

Alongside the painful development of awareness, (many of us are familiar with the feeling of being at a loss for effective action in the face of an overwhelming problem such as climate change), there is a call to political action and for each in our own way to break down the walls which make us suffer. We are even shown the ultimate state of our inhumane ability to exploit the earth rapaciously, make war, and otherwise behave unconscious- ly. This is reflected in the heart of a person *"which does not beat."* And here, with the authority of the poem's dedication, the poet confronts and calls out perpetrators. Yet in the face of all, the *"burning world"* that the Buddha illuminated centuries ago, we are encouraged to *"Soar over the edge, and make a beloved circle."* The poet recommends everything from *"flash mobs"* to *"oc- cupying the corners of fascist madness."* Ultimately there is a firm faith that each of us has the capacity to train ourselves to access a wise heart and use ourselves in response to the world. *"Can you leap beyond all walls of the mind/ and into your deepest heart, arrive."*

By the poem's closing lines, the sorrowful image of the bitter almond hedge has given way to a cinematic rendering of the archetypal Tree of Life, the Bodhi Tree of Awakening. Nourished by the waters of compassion, it holds all of life in Nature's own slow, majestic wisdom and finally we find release from our small, grieving selves. The *"heart which patiently waits"* fi- nally arrives in the eternal present where it can *"know the measure of courage/ and the wellspring of our heart/ from which we sip nectar."* Finally the heart is freed from suffering by its capacity *"to love fiercely every living thing."*

Cathy Wickham
San Francisco September 2013

The Heart of
The Prajna Paramita Sutra

The noble Bodhisattva Avalokitesvara, while absorbed in the deep practice of *prajna paramita*, looked upon the five *skandhas* and seeing they were empty of intrinsic-existence, crossed beyond all suffering and difficulty.

She said, "Here, Shariputra,

form is emptiness, emptiness is form.

Form itself is emptiness; emptiness itself is form.

So too are feeling, cognition, karmic patterning, and consciousness.

Here, Shariputra, all *dharmas* are empty of characteristics. They are not produced, not destroyed, not defiled, not pure, and they neither increase nor diminish.

Therefore, Shariputra, in emptiness there is no form, feeling, cognition, karmic patterning, or consciousness; No eyes, ears, nose, tongue, body, or mind; no sights, sounds, smells, tastes, feeling, thoughts, or *dharmas*; no element of perception up to and including no conceptual consciousness; no ignorance or ending of ignorance, including no old age and death or ending of old age and death. There is no suffering, no cause, no relief, no path, no knowledge, and no attainment or non-attainment.

Therefore, Shariputra, because nothing is attained, bodhisattvas rely on *prajna paramita* and live without walls of the mind. Without walls of the mind, they are not afraid, and they leave distorted dream-thinking far behind. Ultimately Nirvana!

All buddhas, past, present and future through reliance on *prajnaparamita,* realize unexcelled, perfect enlightenment. Therefore, know that *prajnaparamita* is a great spiritual mantra, a mantra of great magic, a supreme mantra, equal to the unequalled. It can heal all suffering. It is true and not false. That is why the mantra of *prajna paramita* is spoken like this:

Gate Gate Paragate Parasamgate Bodhi Svaha!

The Heart of
The Bitter Almond Hedge Sutra

When Avalokitesvara was immersed in the profound unknowing womb of wisdom, s/he illuminated the five *skandhas* and saw that they were all empty and crossed beyond all difficulty. She bowed unto the Earth and it became her body. *Shariputra*, be here now, always. Emptiness is not empty because of wonderful existence; sacred existence doesn't exist because of emptiness. Return to your original heart, leave distorted dream-thinking far behind, leap beyond fear, and live without walls of the mind. Always remember your deepest heart is true, and not false. Praise to the one gone beyond, gone beyond the beyond, gone into intimate oneness and completion.

Gate, Gate, Paragate, Parasamgate, Bodhi Svaha.

1.

All dead people and all animals walk one path. Dead gemsbok, dead ostriches, dead Boers, and dead Bushmen all walk that path. The dead walk a path that is a Bushman's path; it is a path that is the First Koisan's path.

Things that are flesh are those, which dying, must go away; But I who am the moon, I do this; I return.

//Kabbo said this.

In the times before we arrived
lions stalked slowly.
Their hot breath alive
with the essence of stars.

Moonlight heart beats
in slow, peeling night
spirals
that twist like floating mobiles
over a baby's cot,
winding their airless way
through pressed down pages
of woven history.

Floating, unspoken sounds
of our abandoned heart
grow silently into a wall
with sides and edges
that push up to skin
and differences
that set apart,
so we no longer float,
or flow,
or belong to each other.

On each side,
where difference
crushes down,
the wall reaches up,
and within its shadow
partial history
of burnt braai.
Its smoke-poisoned fumes
of circle beer talk
smother our hurting heart.

The hopeful schoolboy,
his polished shoes already scuffed,
balances on the curb's edge
outside Pep Store.
His school shirt,
sleeves rolled up to ebony elbows,
buttons lost.
His bag hangs heavy from faded straps
pressed into his shoulders
slumped down
through hands pushed
into empty pockets.
He looks up the dusty road
with expectant gaze
for his difficult future to arrive.

We have arrived into harsh dreams
where floating lines
drag into abrupt corners,
tense and perilous
narrow words
like "subhuman"
that we slide along edgewise.

2.

A sorcerer watches the doings of the night as he sleeps. Although he is sleeping, he watches, and he knows as he sleeps what things walk about in the night, things that we who are not shamans do not know: he watches while he is asleep to protect his people from the things that come to kill them. Dia!kwan said this.

1666. The Bitter Almond Hedge arrives for our future.
I planted it to ensure against contamination.
Jan van Riebeeck's righteous resolution,
his stubborn solution
defining "safe" illusions
at a price we now know,
but do wish to talk about.
That prickled circle
upholds distance
from our muted heart
with words like
"these people"
as finger points to skin.

Each side of the hedge we edge.
We slide down,
we inch up, and we recoil.
We spin like gigantic mobiles
in the black, velvet night.
At daybreak,
with our faint hearts,
we peer over the edge.
But most of all,
we get used to it.

We lean comfy against the wall
as it divides,
like stone lines dragged

4

across our abandoning heart,
which twists into what was agreed upon.
But we can't remember why.

From the satisfied side,
that floating
haunts our night dreams
with wishful hope
laced around fear's barb;
its parched desert cacti.

A quiet and calm moon
soothes termites scurrying
and hyena stalking,
while night infinity
dissolves our certainty.

From burnt red earth our wagons roll
where protea, grass and mountains rise
and waterfalls cascade down to the ocean.

Salt waves reach into crashing memories,
while playing on the sea wall,
a young girl, yet to learn,
the full force of history.

3.

The men had said to them that they would not stay away long, but they had not come back after three nights in the veldt. Therefore, the women sent the crow, the crow flew away, he searched until he saw the men's vultures. The men were lying dead among the vultures, and the crow went back. He told the women the men would not return because the raiders had killed them. Dia!kwan said this.

And just as the bitter almond hedge
sent us marching to some strange beat
through lonely landscapes
in our tight red coats,
where sweat from heat
and dreams longing
thread estranged days.

And so it became war.
We killed those non-humans.
We did it again and again
with stamped permits; three springbok,
one lion, and two Bushmen.
The Bible said so.
And we,
crazy neat,
rational and civilized,
superior and aloof
White Right
to do so.

On God's side
Europe of old
winkled a thought
from its pickled brain
and for everyone's sake
set about to plant, "trade"

secure, ward off, beat down,
push up and away
into that dark shadowy other
that keeps you;
Queen of Underworld
Mouth of Mysteries
Africa…far, far, away.

Hier staan ons voor
die Heilige God
van hemel en aarde…
To God we entrust our survival.

Far away at daybreak,
we banish that floating feeling
behind our perfectly constructed wall
and crush it beneath our desolate heart
sutra of desertion.
We too know the cost
of our land.
We were slaughtered,
betrayed and bludgeoned,
left alone and bleeding.

Dis 'n graf in die gras,
Dis n' vallende traan.
Dis al.

It's a grave in the grass
It's a falling tear.
That's all/ everything.

4.

The mistress beat me; she said I was not washing the dishes. She did not see I was working nicely with her cups so as not to break them. She pushed me down, trampled me, kicked me, and beat me. When I came home, I was still warm, but the wind was cold. I lost my breath and my heart fell; I could scarcely breathe because my heart had fallen. She said I was lazy, but my heart had fallen. Han!kasso said this of Doortje – wife of !Gubbu prisoner number 4638 of the Breakwater Convict Station..

African woman stands firm her ground
in the shadows of my dreams.
The wind blows her milk through
my sleepless nights
that flow past
the river Zambezi
over which the ancestors crossed.
Hollow beating at my windowpane,
through a starless night.
A large orange moth.

Dawn rising slowly,
red disc and lion stalking;
running from dream to dream.
Time of a different order, Afrika.

Promise what we might,
drift under night water
and weep by the evening willows.
Whisper over far oceans
the strange secrets found.
The marketplace is overflowing
in exile from our hinterland,
while our departure arrives
at the patient stall of Africa.

In this coming,
memories of church bells
and primrose lawns
crowd into our longing.

The full bloom rose,
imported thorn
and petal, white curling brown,
drops to where we meet our fear.

Drive alert through Johannesburg.
Why this despair now we have it made?
In our Mercedes we steer quickly through
red lights and all we can buy, and more.
More for completeness
to fill the gap
that yawns open in a moment
of non-ambition, of non-competition.

Our polished persona in place
holds this world together to create distance
from the man with a cardboard sign.
Homeless, Please Help!

Put the car in gear and accelerate
to our razor-wire frontier cocoon
where we stay immune.
Turn on the TV and forget
there ever was
the pain of home sickness.

5.

The hammerkop cries because the star has fallen; it has come to tell us one of our people has died. For the stars know the time at which we die. "Fly off to the Orange River and plunge your story into it, for we know what you have come to tell us," the people say to it. Your story should be in the river with its shining stars. But the hammerkop is not a thing that deceives people; what it knows, it has seen in the water where it lives. The things that happen of other people, of things in the sky and in its darkness the stars look like fires that burn. Dia!kwain said this.

Through the mind's labyrinth
we slip-slide
and disappear
down our cut-through heart.
This slope into forgetfulness
draws up the floating wound
that heaves under our neat exterior
where the wail of a beast,
that knows no soothing,
weeps hot pain.
It circles and circles
looking for fresh meat
ripping through
shreds of coherency.
Shards of heart
scatter to the icy winds
during the darkening night.

Oh night of no stars;
of no rescue;
of lost things;
of uncertain horizons;
of souls turning,
floating, twisting,
and plummeting,
so we can't sense the holding.

At dawn light we lean into the wall
that comforts with its tight breath
and thin vein of reasons
that catch agreements in a flick of an eye.
The currency of our careful clan cohesion.

I like
he would always say,
to have my ducks in a row.

We like
to prevent that floating feeling
from haunting our heart's corner.
So keep "these people"
on the other side of my mind,
far from the fated pull
that stalks,
beautiful and powerful,
my banished dreams.

6.

Death: *A colonizing technology, a mastering technology, a parting from the land, and Gwai-ttu went to take a beast from a farmer but was shot and died on the hunting ground.*

The last Bushman.
Found with artist's powder
tied to his waist.
1921.

Our lands,
so quiet without us,
grieve.
Our sacred soul-connection
severed from
our eland and grasses
that blow in the hot, dry winds, alone.

Uzimkulu, your water hastens
over rocks, plants and dreams
of unity.
A stream of time
is this moment only
and millions of years
mighty Drakensberg,
you witness the sun setting
on tribe, empire and queen
while unseen we cry into the earth.
Here is our faint song,
the weary arrow of our phantom
reaching down from night stars.
Our spirit is saying,
"this was our land."

As we are killed,
your soul too
ebbs away.

Left to the mercy of genocide's machination
we were drained down into a corner of weakness.
Trying to sustain a self
not dependent on others,
on blessed Earth,
made us empty.

We were weaned on grotesque machinery,
on industrial, numb rape.
Conquering and ransomed
humans became engines
striding forth, disembodied and perplexed.
Their shiny gaze and traumatized hearts
sway under corporate personhood.

Now we sign ourselves away
to walk the nights alone
morphing into hollow ghosts.

This, our lost soul,
beats down and down
into a narrow passage of lonely wandering,
where we mindfully pick up the pieces
along the path of our broken heart
that tries to find a way home.

7.

"I greet you, Mother. I am still your little one, and I am still well. And I still live here—a little while here. My youngest daughter is working for a master at Graskraal, and my second daughter, too. I cry for them, I long to see them. My sons have gone away. I wait, I wait, but I do not know when they shall visit me again. Mother, your daughter has not one child living with her; she feels like an orphan. I weep because I am an orphan. Tell me, have you seen your son, your brother, my sister? Your daughter greets you—and I still think of you, my mother." Rachel, wife of Guiman, said this. (One of the last messages of the /Xam.)

She in her lost need,
ripe for plunder,
you broke into her body
and invaded her soul
to deliver your fatal wound.

See what lay beneath your charm.
Ingratiating words
claiming loyalty
slip easily
from your glazed smile.

Your predator nature,
serial, hidden and chained
to your secret lack of worth,
feeds your need to dominate,
to sexually excruciate,
to exploit powerlessness
in the graveyard of empty souls.

Claiming spiritual superiority,
your aloof gaze of no good god
injects poison into the open legs

of the trust you cynically invite.
You thrashed the garden growing,
you lied to rescue your darkness,
without a care for the devastation you sow.

Sociopathic sex
slumbering and urgent,
survival and death
sweeping through love
semen and blood
mixes ancient thrill
and conquering our frail flesh,
mortal flesh,
succumbing to predator HIV.

She, poisoned Earth body,
immune no more,
laid waste
in fields of the usurpers' dominion.

Swaying grass chewed over
and over by the goddesses cow.
Rape racked raw,
she produces our liquid soothing
mixed with Monsanto Matricide
seeds of GMO.
One cup into Sunday's milk pudding
while asleep in TV lounges of puzzlement.
Outside, the stars we barely know.

8.

A star is like our heart at the time in which we die, for it shoots, it falls down when our heart falls down, falling from the throat, from the hollow of the throat; it shoots when we die, for it knows the time when we die. It takes our hearts away.
Said Dia!kwain

Pause and breathe…fully.
A truce of hopeful covenant
seeded from the devastation
of mad narcissistic lust
to frack, extract
tar sands
main lining
farm lands
stolen and hammered
blown off mountain tops,
stoking grandiose greed
that crashes against emerging
wild and violent protest.

Finally the bandages off
and the raw,
stinking,
suppurating,
gash rushes
through the trapdoor
we tried to close shut
over our tight, pounding heart.

Breathe again…truly.
Try to pause longer
as we all fall
like ballet dancers
with no reference points.

Floating down,
we whirl round and around
through layers of sanity
that dissolve quickly behind us.
Glide and fall over our intimate
heart-beating
strewn to the side
as we crash against the wall.

- In the dusty township, our song of liberation;
- Beating drums when you come back;
- To electric razor wire Jo'burg hedge;
- Press panic button, quick, open;
- Away from suspicious youth;
- Pushing cart in Golden Gate Park;
- On the way to the Philharmonic Orchestra;
- Drop a few cents;
- As Wall Street deregulates;
- Sinking New Orleans;
- White suburbia watches on flat-screen TV;
- Army-clad guards through the night;
- Security fence scars Holy Land;
- Cain and Abel, stones and tanks;
- The new wall rises:
- Iraq, Green Zone myth;
- Arab spring uncoils;
- Crowds Mumbai train station;
- Pakistani youth, shoot and shoot;
- Up cocaine in London alley;
- Colombia drug barons hide;
- Behind walls of USA home;
- Foreclosure, sociopathic, greed;
- Koch Brothers buy media and army;
- To crush women and children;
- To control fossil fuel crack;
- And hidden earth bomb;
- Chernobyl and Fukushima;

- Star fish melt and rip themselves apart:
- Mother tried, father died;
- As Planet Earth is pushed to demise;
- Behold; This is the time of Shiva;
So shall we...shall we, all die?
Is this how it ends?

Gate, gate, paragate, parasamgate, bodhi svaha.

9.

At what place did you grow up? You must tell me, old woman. Tell me your place's name, the place at which you grew up, the place at which you lived when you were still a child; and of what people have you made your companions? Tell me, you must tell me the names of those who are your people. Tell me the name of your father and the name of your mother, and those who are your children; and what is your name, old woman, what are you called? /Han≠kasso said this.

Our names are one.

Move with that floating feeling
and let it erupt into words
of radical revolution
that rise along our bone spine
finding shape for a pain
that haunts and ripples
like thundering Orcs,
their cynical knives twisting
under soft skin struggling
to stand
against psychosis
and callous disdain
ripping apart coherency
and our beauty, sweet, soft breath.

Pushed beneath our flayed,
thin skin,
stretched over tired bones
with our wound whispered,
the wall that vanquishes
collapses into
our daytime task.
To name truth words
that spawn web memes

exposing
corporate planted hedges
of bitter ecocide.
Their venomous fruits
eviscerating sanity
in programmed denial
that set hell free.

Do not wander that twilight alone,
where a haunting wail rolls
along pathways that lead nowhere.
There, you will lose your power.
Try not to spiral down.
Instead, in a sun-drenched meadow
by the bank of a sleepy river
with friends that ask no words,
try this simple task
to ignite your vocation
of sacred communion.
Try to stand up.
Try to hold true,
to hold,
holy body and soul together.

Hold together so we can navigate
the floating gyroscope
as it spirals towards a flower
perched on a rock face
in dense forest donga
rich with pulsing sounds
and delicate laced lichen.

Her petals entice
a turquoise red sunbird

to drink full its desire,
as shadows gather the blazing sun
into chilled caves
of long, gone First Peoples
where baboon and eland
drink crystal water,
iridescent and most pure,
flowing down sculptured caverns
through exploded volcanic
rock art shamanic portal.

Torrents of rain draw in
ribbons of violet, white lightening
impregnating the sloping valleys
with crashing thunder
that rolls through jagged peaks
to the riverbed below
where a solitary Zulu,
herding cattle,
grasps his *sqwayi* with gnarled fingers.

His woolly hat and blue coat,
stained with the weight
of defeated history.

10.

A quiet knock at the door invites him inside. Sitting on wobbly plastic chairs, his bleak story told with hushed dread. Revenge exacted by his girlfriend leaves him HIV infected. Outside on the stoep, reflected hot sun glistens on the skin of a green-striped snake; its dislocated jaw swallowing a screaming mouse. As it slithers away, the storm breaks and rain splatters onto the dry earth, releasing its sweet smell. The day Sipho told about Nkosi.

The sons are gone.
Their spirits roam
in the twilight
of AIDS body,
thin, sick body,
no way to say body,
young body, gone bad body.

The daughters are gone,
barely breathing
falling down body,
young, raped, girl body,
HIV shame body,
hidden anguish body.

Ancestors call them back
before they want to go body.
They drift, wild with loss
softly crumbling in decimated homes
but find no one
to meet them there.

Millions of spirits...
They roam saying, why?
Why?
Why me?

11.

The wind does thus when we die, our own wind blows; for we, who are human beings, make clouds when we die. Therefore, the wind does thus when we die, the wind makes dust, because it intends to blow, taking away our footprints, with which we had walked about while we still had nothing the matter with us; and our footprints, which the wind intends to blow away, would otherwise still lie plainly visible. For, it would seem as if we still lived. Therefore, the wind intends to blow, taking away our footprints. So said Dia!kwain.

Ancestors roam townships
of people left behind,
where those with no footprints
try to find a foothold.

Hostel eGoli
City of Gold.
His name is Freedom.
His taxi ride is from the Mines.
Ten hours stacked together
as his chest pain intensifies.

sawubona, unjani, sikhona
His long ago injured soul
stares blank through downcast eyes.
His sinewy arms with protruding veins
and worn, vacant hands.
His sagging skin
pulled over his thirty-year-old frame
planted into Wellington boots
for the long walk to the door.
Boss, lend me a hundred rand.

There was lifting him off the road,
a battle-fallen drunk.

The three hundred rand for prison bail.
His striding up the mountain to douse a runaway fire.
The time he thrust out his hand with crumpled notes,
Boss, your money back.
And the time he got shot dead,
five bullets into his never smiling head.
The gun shoved to his enemy
by his
oh-so-lovely
girlfriend.

Wonder how love turns to hate
and hate boils astringent lies
that burn and entwine truth
in the doomed wilderness
of crazy-making enemies.
The wall secretes betrayal,
as segregation's most bitter legacy.

Once a friend.
Now he twists and tricks
along pathways that descend
into a mesh of mad deception
to grab the "prize"
as it evaporates in his cold,
calculating hands.
Here, projected shadows
generate hard returns
of denial's journey.
All the way to the embattled end.

12.

Its name is ≠Koaxa, while the Europeans call it Haarfontein; and it was at Haarfontein that Smoke's Man saw the wind. He saw the wind but thought it was a !kuerre-!kuerre bird, and therefore, he threw a stone at it, and it burst into wind, it burst out blowing, it blew hard, it blew fiercely.. It raised the dust, and it flew away and went into a mountain hole: and he, Smoke's Man, being afraid, went home. The wind was once a man, but he became a bird and wore feathers on his skin and went to live on a mountain. He became a bird and no longer walked, but he flew. He wakes up early and he leaves his mountain and he flies about, he flies about, about, about, about, as he flies to eat, and then he returns, he returns there to sleep; and because he feels that his feathers used to blow, he, too, blows. They were the wind and therefore they blew, and he, the son of the wind, is now a bird. So said. / Han≠kasso.

Leaving.
We are leaving.
Shredded and raw heart seeks calm shore.

We dream another shore waiting
and we need to know how to go.
Not flights of fancy
of awakenings' glitz
floating eloquences
of enlightenment.
Tongue bright with witty insight
flowing from throat to head
shaping realities of transcendence,
while in the core of burning *samsara*
swirls of emotion
float free
on upward circling perceptions
divorcing themselves from our heart connection.

Ascenders into the light,
we are descending before you.

25

An exhausted pile of bones
smouldering in cold ash
from words sliding sideways
in mega churches
preaching
spiritual dissonance reunion.

There is no heaven in the sky.
No *nirvana* apart from *samsara*.
No paradise virgin to your violence reward.
And no Planet B.

So sit the night patiently through
and gather your wayward mind.
Take up your own power
as in your heart
is the earth's body
and all bodies,
the stars, mountains, oceans,
flowers, trees, cities and moon.

Sit until dawn, without flying to the light.
Instead, plunge your life
into your unfathomable yearning
so you can be pulled to the intimacy
that this direct path heralds
within each beating heart
where every precious breath
redeems your lost soul.

And when preachers promise a far off place
in lucid rationale,

challenge them
with your honest voice.

"Can you dissolve the walls of the mind
and into your undivided heart arrive
to stand up fierce
for our earth
for her all living beings?
If not, then leave me
and your flights of fancy behind."

Because from common ground
we move from birth into destiny
and death dream reality
where bone ash wait.

Because all is possibility
with no substance found.
Particles of no-thing-ness
transform into each other
in universal systems
of potentiality
where space, time, matter and light
forever melt like waking dreams.

13.

Be careful as when crossing an iced-over stream. Alert as a warrior in enemy territory. Courteous as a guest. Fluid as melting ice. Shapable as a block of wood. Receptive as a valley. Clear as a glass of water. Kind-hearted as a grandmother. Tolerant, disinterested, amused and dignified as a king. Can you remain unmoving till the right action arises by itself? Immersed in the wonder of the Tao, you can deal with whatever life brings you, and when death comes, be ready. So said Lao Tzu

We are not ready.
Moving, we already left.
Heart-beats pacing doubts:
Where to go?
What to do?
What about funds?
What about friends?
Where?
What?
Why?
How?
How to keep afloat
In a Diaspora of imperfect landings.

Emptiness is form.
Which form, what place?
Choose and move.
America, England, Australia?
hamba khale, PfP
Pack for Perth
we go…lining up for X-rays,
vaccinations and AIDS test
at Durban hospital.
So sad, said the lady,
so sad
to see everyone go.

Leaving.
Taste the moment
when essences of soul
imprinted with a million memories
cease their flighty hovering and settle
into this deepest core
of your aching heart.
You will know,
white ocean foam,
an *umlungu* lost in the dark,
what it is to have been here
inside the shattered soul of Afrika
with salt tears pressed from your guilty shackle.

But still,
try to celebrate
the exquisite perfection of all parts
lighted by a shaft of blessings
that was there,
within your torn landscape,
all along.

There is no suffering,
no origin of suffering,
no end of suffering,
and no path.
Gate gate, paragate, parasamgate.

So breathe deeply
and take a moment
here and now
to sit and recall
this authentic gift.
The love that moves

to death chants
like an African drum
beating in your breast
as each ones breath
vibrates into flesh
drinking breast milk
that tastes blood, AK-47s
and mournful lullabies.

Try to soften and breathe in
conflicted streets where violence roams
and where the rolling hills are sodden
with downpour hailstone lightning.

Allow the cries that tumble across
the peaceful, vast veldt
of mountainous struggles
to flow through you.

Let the hot sun melt your shield
as you walk the dusty street of
warm, black, skin softly smiles
where the boy with satchel and dreams
wanders the thin, wishful highway
of no jobs.

Kneel on this unforgiving ground
and ease into a pulsing life force
that turns us together saying,
Relax, child, and drink from my ancient breast.

Raise the brave new flag
unfurled kite of free spirit
with bold colour
declaring dreams,
still to arrive.

Your voice, iAfrika,
is unmistakable in its hopeful sound.
But you won't let us relax.

Every day
your hot breath rattles
our fear tune
as we flirt with your invitation
to live more fully
in the nourishing belly
of your hungry domain.

So drift along now,
on the white cloud and dusk star rising,
as the red-streaked night
sweeps in indigo and gold
mixing into rain drops from the passing storm
that runs down the mountain
to the riverbed below
to be drunk by cattle, leopard, humans,
and a crimson flower
balancing perfectly in the breeze.

14.

1894 – Government agents started to divide the Hopi, People of Peace, into two opposed factions, and reported: *"In the pueblo of Oraibi, there are two factions called by the Whites the "Friendlies," and the "Hostiles." The Friendlies sent their children to school and are willing to adopt civilized ways; the Hostiles, under the bad influence of shamans, believe that the abandonment of old ways will be followed by drought and famine."* So said Sun Bôw True Brother. *Hopi Katsi et Tuwa Eyesni...* May the Way of Peace Prevail on Earth.

Enlightenment is simple.
Enlightenment is a Rubik's Cube.
Enlightenment is not what you think.
Enlightenment is a word.
Enlightenment is intimacy with all things.

Some things devastate
in the night-time;
where dark dreams drop us down
to our knees and pray.

Two a.m. moonbeams
draw in distant American warplanes.
Nightmare treachery tracks
enemies of the state
of extraordinary rendition.
So we can Drone and Gitmo forgotten dreamers.

We, who float far from our original
homeland security
siren as Twin Towers
fall down truth
into conniving, twisted lies
in steel girders

shipped quickly
to China.

You without heartbeat,
you know what you did.
And you know what you want.
You kill freedom.
You kill wilderness.
Your skull drips black oily blood,
and your body moves
to a false tune.
You are doctor death in a mask
of tight trickery
and war crimes not addressed.

The night of darkness,
the night of no stars,
the night of no returning moon
in the desert of our wanting.
Iraq laid to waste.

Inside and outside
there is no form, feeling, cognition,
no eyes, ears, nose, body, or mind.
no mind
no mind
no mind

15.

Thus, I heard. On one occasion, the Blessed One was living at Gaya, together with a thousand Bhikkhus and Bhikkhunis. "Bhikkhus and Bhikkhunis, all is burning. And what is the all that is burning? "The eye is burning, forms are burning, eye-consciousness is burning, eye-contact is burning...

The ear is burning, sounds are burning...
The nose is burning, odors are burning...
The tongue is burning, flavors are burning...
The body is burning, tangibles are burning...

The mind is burning, ideas are burning, mind-consciousness is burning, mind-contact is burning, also whatever is felt as pleasant or painful or neither painful nor pleasant, and that too is burning. Burning with what? Burning with the fire of lust, with the fire of hate, with the fire of delusion. I say it is burning with birth, aging, and death. Burning with sorrow, lamentation, pain, grief, and despair. So said the Buddha.

Just know the feeling in the feeling.
Is it pleasant, unpleasant, or neutral?
Bud-dho, attend within each heartbeat.
Bud...with the in breath.
Dho...with the out breath.
Direct mindful awareness to feeling.
Pleasant, unpleasant, or neutral...?

It is unpleasant.
Consuming fire of outrage
shoots searing sensations
into our flesh core.
Frozen grief at deceitful ruin
aches every living cell.
Weighted stones
of dreaded despair
pull the heart down

34

through each vertebra
into softening tissue
and oxygenated blood
pumping pain.

Chemical dissonance
surges into brain coordination
and scrambles sanity.
Trauma releases into the world.

The beast has no holding.
It roams and scavenges
the desecrated, rotting flesh
of grandiose structures
that peel away from
our faded, fast, Capitalist Gods
who abandon us all
in the end.

Here, enlightenment lands
like a sick thump to the stomach.

At night we track mala beads
along the wild stations of our heart
so we can know
the lost islands of our soul,
like animals at a dry water hole.

16.

Earth is rapidly headed towards a catastrophic breakdown if humans don't get their act together. The world is headed towards a tipping point marked by extinctions and unpredictable changes. The Earth is going to be a very different place. We are to be pushed through the eye of the needle of political strife, economic strife, war, and famine. So say the scientists.

This being human is a guest house
of toxic dumped wastelands.
Every morning a new arrival
where life grows no more.
Meet them at the door laughing
at our insane leap to death.
Or screaming
through the abandoned stations of heart.
Or collapsed on the sofa
shooting up the drug of our choice
so we can forget
and not feel
our dissolving into oblivion.
This
is…is not,
is not human.
We are not humane any more.

We, the machine,
testify against ourselves
as our future screams towards us.
Machiavellian corporate psychopaths
swarm through every cell
like millions of dead bees
of media words
spewing onto streets of choking cities.

Our floating dear heart
knots and twists
downwards
pulled by the gravitational
collapsing empire
of the wall's inevitable seduction
into total destruction.

Stranded people struggle
to pull the needle out
from raised veins
of unhappiness
as they fall
under the belly
of the crazed
fossil fuel dinosaur

Earth haunts another waking night
weeping her beloved species
disappearing.
Terror from the slaughterhouse
reaps horrific carnage
of concentration camp
vicious violence
feeding sadomasochistic depravity
of no human, anymore.

Animals as objects twisted
into iron bar cages of no mercy.
Artificially inseminated, castrated,
ejaculated, plucked, crushed, torn, trashed,
boiled, and skinned alive.

Our human heart flees
the intimacy of all things
as a terror tsunami of black karma arrives.

Good-bye tigers;
Good-bye lions;
Good-bye elephants;
Good-bye rhinos;
Good-bye orang-utan;
Good-bye humble bumblebee;
Good-bye coral reefs;
Good-bye albatross;
Good-bye Amazon River;
Good-bye Arctic Circle;
Good-bye us all…

Hello raging, elemental storms of the world's end.

17.

Nirvana: *cessation of burning, the taintless, the truth, the other shore, the subtle, the everlasting, the invisible, the undifferentiated, the deathless, peace, the blest, safety, exhaustion of craving, the wonderful, the marvellous, non-hostility, freedom, the island, the shelter, the harbour, the refuge, the beyond, the end.* So said the Buddha.

So pause at the gate of no returning
at the edge
of the hedge
end game.

Here *Shariputra*, balances perilous survival
twisting in the wind of our whims.
Here *Shariputra*, the brave leap of reclamation.
Our deepest heart implores it,
with liquid, fluid prayer.
So turn the mad mind around
from its callous scalpel to the world.

From the collapsing furnace of known lands
fierce and urgent cries mop up denial.
Millions sign: All Out Now!
Quick, before it's too late
to walk again
in the rose-scented garden
where your soul patiently waits
among shattered fragments
of the empire
to break down your wall
of small expectations
and from nightmares
pull you awake.

Here is the faith of wild warriors
Who leave dream-thinking far behind.
Who leap beyond the walls of the mind.
Who know the intimacy of all things.
And who return to this, our human
that feels the scream
in each mindful moment
and chooses
to soften.
To breathe the mystery.
To enter the unknown gate.
To love fiercely every living thing,
right down to the last blade of grass.

Quick, time, any time.
Here and now will do.
Move beyond your walled pastimes
to join the Awakening.
Time yourself out
from the needle of craving
and boogie down with intense
flamenco, disciplined passion
so we can crash the machine.

Soar over the edge
on the breath of our heart's sorrow
and make a beloved circle
outside the wall
where the storehouse of untamed dreams
will decolonize our mind.

On the dark horse
of their unfolding,
the warriors march in tune

to her victorious soft truth,
unwrapping our heart
it shatters
tight psychopathic masks
and the intensity of our madness
as we upturn
the cavern of denial
and the collapsing cave
of our ancestral wounds,
over which we leap.

We might pray, wail,
and sometimes fail.
But here we fall at the feet
of that with no name,
which has all names printed
into our authentic heart
woven into each part
of joyous, sane, and connected
primordial ease.
Do it now—if not now…when?

Death of the planet won't wait for another time.
The "perhaps" and the "maybe."

18.

Those who set forth on this path should give birth to this thought: "Whatever living beings there are, in whatever realms, I shall work to free them. And though I free living beings, not a single being is liberated. And why not? No one can be a bodhisattva who creates the perception of 'a self,' of 'a being,' of 'a life span,' or of 'a soul.'" So teaches the Diamond Sutra.

Still, if someone should lean towards you
on a cold, forsaken night
inviting you to leave your castle wall,
lean with her into your deepest hope.
Because the storm is coming.

I dream a wild forest
of parrots and monkeys.
Maybe one day,
I will return.

Do you feel the ardent scream
in our heart molten agony
rising on fire
from the torture of the Earth?

Eaarth dust walkers
together
through the tangle,
we stumble
to return
wild shamanic power
of the hearts
pure peace pulse.

In quiet release of identification,
from the fired and wired
off-sync brain
merged with the machine,
prajna intuitive intelligence
of the deep
rewires.
She
pours living truth into us
and leads our way home.

- True Heart home;
- Soft Heart home;
- Fierce Heart home;
- Generous Heart home;
- Merciful Heart home;
- Swift Protection Heart;
- Invincible Courage Heart;
- True Refuge Heart;
- Destroyer of Negativity Heart;
- Bliss and Equanimity Heart;
- Remover of Sorrow Heart;
- Transformer of Poison Heart;
- Serene Peace Heart;
- Distribution of Wealth Heart;
- Impeccable Virtue Heart;
- Joy and Laughter Heart;
- Sublime Intelligence Heart;
- Creative Wisdom Heart;
- Worthy of Honour Heart;
- Foundation in Freedom Heart:
- Radiant Health Heart;
- Ferocious Compassion Heart;
- All Victorious Heart;
- Complete Enlightenment Heart;
- Aware Heart;
- Present Heart;
- Avalokitesvara, Hands and Eyes Heart.

Gate, Gate, Paragate
This mantra is true and not false.
Mother of the Buddhas.
Matrix of creation.
Empty of all distinctions.
Your true heart hears all beings,
their beginning and their end.
Your true heart is not the seer or seen,
and it is both.
Just this!
Parasamgate Bodhi Svaha.

Everything now means nothing,
except how much
you reclaim your human
that loves your life
your Earth
your all other living beings
and every flower pushing through concrete
on your way to work.

Because this is the moment you've waited for.
The moment for wild prayer,
flash mobs,
and for occupying the corners of fascist madness.
Sit your ground.
Stake your truth.
And should you be brave,
then shout out
to the far corners of the walls
until the force of our sound together
demolishes every carefully positioned brick.

19.

I feel that tonight I shall die, for I am wounded by an arrow, and the wound is telling me that I shall die. The bite of the wound is fierce, and the mouth of the wound does not heal, but it swells and throbs so that my flesh aches and I burn with pain and feel my heart falling. I know I shall not see the break of another day, for my heart feels I am to die, and I cannot bear to think of the smell of springbok. But as for you, you must look after the children, you must keep them with you, you must keep them beside you, you must not take your eye from them, you must not give them away to strangers, you must keep a good fire so that the cold does not kill them. And though I will be dead, I will think of you and the children. I will still think of you, and wonder whether you are warm and have food. I shall not speak to you again, I shall not speak to you in the darkness of the night, but you shall fetch wood and make up a fire and sit beside me and watch over me and take care of me as I writhe by the fire, for the time of death has come, and the time for talking is over: I speak to you, holding up your heart so that you may understand. Told by //Kabbo

Time with relentless harvesting
your precious human life
is short.
As all life
gathers proof of our faith
through the pilgrimage of the night
that tests the grounds of our being,
so we may know
the measure of courage
and the wellspring of our heart,
from which we sip nectar.

Just as the brown, striped bug
drinks from the white elderflower,
and the orange, thin-winged butterfly
skips through ochre grasses,
and the grey, knowing wolves
move through cold, white snow,
and the rhinos through dry, bush veldt, go

as lions stalk impala
along the river slow.

Slow is the Earth's rhythm,
deep and unfathomable in our collective soul.
The rhythm of the days tick-tock,
winding through the web of our connection
of Internet consumption
where we search what we hope to know.

Because to truly know is to not know.
And to not know
is so much evidence of where faith can go.

It is like a great regal tree growing in the rocks and sand of barren wilderness. When the roots get water, the branches, leaves, flowers, and fruits will all flourish. The regal tree of enlightenment growing in the wilderness of birth and death is the same. All living beings are its roots; all buddhas and bodhisattvas are its flowers and fruits. By serving all beings, by serving this great Earth, by pouring the water of living, gentle, and fierce compassion, together we will embody the flowers and fruits of our true awakening. And even when the realms of empty space are exhausted, the realms of living beings are exhausted, the karmas of living beings are exhausted, and the afflictions of living beings are exhausted, we will still accord with this, our deepest heart, endlessly, continuously, in thought after thought, without cease. Our body, speech and mind never weary of this service." So says our true heart.

Gate Gate Paragate Parasamgate Bodhi Svaha

Glossary

Sutra – Sutra in Sanskrit (Sutta in Pali which is the scriptural language of Theravada Buddhism), literally means "thread." The Sutras are a large body of texts that record the teachings of the Buddha and Buddhism.

The Heart Sutra: The Heart Sutra is a core text of Mahayana Buddhism. Its full Sanskrit name *Prajñāpāramitā Hrdaya* literally means "The Heart of the Perfection of Transcendent Wisdom." It is particularly popular in Zen schools of Buddhism and is usually recited as part of daily monastic liturgy.

Bodhisattva: Bodhisattva literally means "awake being." A bodhisattva is one who practices to mature an embodied awakening in order to help rescue living beings from suffering. In order to support this process, those practising the bodhisattva path take vows, usually the four bodhisattva vows, to support their spiritual life. The Buddha's enlightenment is traditionally seen as the outcome of the bodhisattva vows and practices he undertook over countless life times.

Avalokitesvara: Avalokitesvara (Sanskrit) "the one who contemplates sound" or "the one who looks over the world" is a mythic being who represents the depth of wisdom and compassion in Buddhist metaphysics. The Chinese transliteration of Avalokitesvara is Kuan Shr Yin which means "the one who contemplates the sounds of the world at ease." It is said that once upon a time Avalokitesvara was so overcome by the suffering of life that his/her head exploded into ten thousand pieces. (Avalokitesvara appears in both masculine and feminine forms, and is said to be able to appear in whatever form is needed in response to suffering.) Avalokitesvara's guru Amitabha Buddha, (who represents the limitless light of pure consciousness), then reconstructed Avalokitesvara, replacing his one head with eleven heads and 10,000 hands and eyes so as to better fulfil her task or rescuing living beings from suffering.

Skandha – Sanskrit (Pali – Kandha) The five skandhas are a teaching framework used by the Buddha to designate what constitutes phenomena, of both the subjective and objective worlds. These are; form, feeling, perception, volition (karmic patterning) and sensory (dualistic) consciousness.

Mantra: This is a Sanskrit word which means "mind protection." A mantra is a phrase, like a short prayer, that is repeated over and over. The repetition of mantra is a spiritual practice that helps the mind focus on the meaning and energy encapsulated within the words of the phrase. Mantras in the Buddhist tradition are connected with the remembrance of teachings as well as expressions of devotion. They also evoke energies of the awakened mind such as wisdom, compassion, clarity, courage, and empowerment.

dharmas: In the context of the Heart Sutra, the word *dharmas* means "things" All phenomena, internal and external, comes together based on the *skandhas* (form, feeling/sensation, cognition/perception, volition/ karmic patterning, sensory/dualistic consciousness), thereby the appearance of *dharmas*, "things," comes to be. However, *dharmas* are inherently insubstantial and therefore not really "things." The Dharma on the other hand has the meaning of both teachings that lead to awakening, and reality, that which is both transcendent and immanent, here and now, ever inviting, timeless and deathless.

/Xam, San, KhoiSan, Bushmen: There are different perspectives on what is the respectful term for the oldest race on Earth that inhabited Southern Africa and who were both hunter-gathers and herders. The first "Bushmen" were called /Xam or "first-there-sitting-people." While the term San, which has the connotation of "outsider" is least preferable, it is still a term commonly used, particularly in the academic community who strive to avoid the perceived derogatory term of Bushmen. The term Khoi usually refers to herders and often the term Khoisan designates the early herders of Southern Africa. While the term Bushmen, given by the first settlers, was indeed derogatory, it is the term used by Bushmen and women themselves and so has been adopted in this poem. Please note that American English uses lower case bushmen, while Anglo-English uses upper case as in Bushmen.

Bushmen Poets: The spelling of the poet's names //Kabbo, Dia!kwan, !Gubbu, Han!kasso, /Xam, /Han≠kasso, //Kabbo uses diacritical marks which designates the phonetic sounds in the San languages. There are various clicks made with the tongue against the palette and side of the mouth. These clicks were adopted into many African languages such as isiZulu and Xhosa.

Boer: Means "farmer" in Afrikaans. It is a term that is sometimes used with derogatory intent, but not always.

Braai: Is Afrikaans for a barbeque. A traditional pastime of white South African social culture is sharing and gathering around a braai.

Red Coats: The British army wore red coats at the time of the Zulu and Boer wars in the late 1800's. The said reason was to hide the blood from wounds. However the red colour against the grass veldt made the many young men, fresh from their homeland of Britain, easy targets.

Hier staan ons voor: These are the opening words of the vow holy to the Afrikaaner nation. The Day of the Vow traces its origin to The Battle of Blood River on 16 December in 1838 when besieged Voortrekkers (Afrikaaners who trekked inland to avoid British rule), took a vow before a battle with the Zulu nation. During the battle it is said a group of about 470 Voortrekkers and their African servants defeated a force of about ten thousand Zulu with the use of their fire power. Only three Voortrekkers were wounded, and some 3,000 Zulu warriors died in the battle. In 1994 it was renamed "Day of Reconciliation" and is observed on December 16th. The vow:

We stand here before the Holy God of heaven and earth, to make a vow to Him that, if He will protect us and give our enemy into our hand, we shall keep this day and date every year as a day of thanksgiving like a sabbath, and that we shall erect a house to His honour wherever it should please Him, and that we will also tell our children that they should share in that with us in memory for future generations. For the honour of His name will be glorified by giving Him the fame and honour for the victory.

Dis 'n graf in die gras: This is the last verse of the haunting poem "Dis Al" written by Jan F.E. Celliers, (1865 –1940), a highly renowned Afrikaaner language poet, essayist, dramatist and reviewer. The poem captures the loneliness and devastation the Afrikaaner faced after the Anglo-Boer wars when they returned home to find their families missing and their farms burnt to the ground by the British.

That's All

Gold,
blue:
veld,
sky;
and one bird wheeling lonely, high -
that's all.
.

An exile come back
from over the sea;
a grave in the grass,
a tear breaking free;
that's all.
(*translated by Guy Butler*)

The last Bushman: This is reference to the area of the Southern Drakensberg, local to the poet's residence, where it was reported that after the tragic killing of the last bushman in the area, he was found to have a collection of the coloured powders, used in rock art, in the tips of antelope horns on his belt.

Uzimkulu: The Uzimkulu River originates in the high mountains on the Eastern border of Lesotho and runs down through the gracious hills of KwaZulu Natal where it meets the ocean at Port Shepstone as a deep and wide sleepy river.

Drakensberg: The Drakensberg (dragon mountains in Afrikaans) are also called the uKhahlamba (barrier of spears in isiZulu.) They form a 1,100 kilometre (700 mile) spine from the Eastern Cape to Mpunglanga, skirting round the Eastern border of Lesotho, and reaching up to 11,000+ feet (3,480 metres) in parts. Altogether there are 35,000 to 40,000 works of Bushmen art, some dating back 2,400 years, in the caves of the Drakensberg. There is anthropological evidence that Bushmen roamed these mountains from 40,000 to 100,000 years ago.

Sqwayi: Is the colloquial Zulu term for a knobkerrie, which is a stick with a heavy end, often carried in rural areas by men as a weapon, a form of protection, and as a traditional cultural object.

Stoep: Afrikaans for veranda or porch.

Hostel eGoli: eGloi, literally meaning "City of Gold," is a common African term for Johannesburg whose rise from the Veldt was entirely due to gold mining. The hostels for miners are notorious as places that engender violence and degradation. Away from their rural homes, wives and families, many miners take a "town wife" which hastened the spread of AIDS into the rural areas that the men return to during holiday times.

Sawubona, unjani, sikhona: This everyday Zulu greetings means, "Hello, how are you?" 'I am well."

Hamba khale: Is isiZulu for "go well."

Samsara: Is a Sanskrit terms which has the meaning of "endless wandering." It refers to the mind always looking for certainty in an uncertain world. Samsara is sometimes depicted as a wheel which ever rotates, driven by ignorance, desire and the laws of karma, (cause and effect.)

Nirvana: (Nibbana in Pali) is the end of the suffering generated from ignorance in regards to the impermanence and insubstantiality of the phenomenal world. Once the mind releases from identification with the *khandas* it tastes the peace of nirvana.

Umlungu: Is an African term for a white person. It is the word for white froth on the ocean. Usually it is meant in a derogatory way, but not always.

Thus have I heard.....Bhikkhus & Bhikkhunis, all is burning: This is taken from The Fire Sermon, (Adittapariyaya Sutta), which is the third discourse of the Buddha after his awakening. The Buddha delivered this teaching to 1,000 fire-worshipping ascetics, turning their minds from religious ritual to a direct practice of awakening, using the metaphor of fire to illuminate the burning nature of greed, aversion and delusion.

Bhikkhus & Bhikkhunis: A Bhikkhu is a Buddhist monk, while a Buddhist nun is called a Bhikkhuni. It means "one who lives on alms food." The author of the poem has added the word Bhikkhuni, where the Suttas rarely include mention of Bhikkhunis, to redress an historical imbalance.

Gate, gate, paragate, parasamgate bodhi svaha: This mantra, which encapsulates the essence of the Heart Sutra, is usually left un-translated or is translated "gone, gone, gone beyond, gone completely beyond, hail the one gone to awakening – so be it!" Basically it is an exclamation of profound faith in the awakened heart which IS, beyond time, space or cognition.

Bud-dho: This is a mantra used in the Thai Forest School as a meditation aid. It is connected to the word Buddha which means "awake." The root of the word Buddha is *bodeti* which has the sense of opening, as the petals of a flower open to the rays of the sun. Buddha/ buddhi/ bodhi have the essential meaning of "knowing." This is not cognitive knowing so much, but intuitive wisdom that is rooted in the vast intelligence of the Dharma. The practice of this mantra guides the mind to rest in the fundamental awareness and presence of the heart.

Know the feeling in the feeling: This is a phrase from The Foundation of Mindfulness Sutta (Satipatthana Sutta), which dates back to the Buddha. It is a graduated teaching which instructs the disciple in the development of mindfulness. This is done by training non judgemental, attentive awareness to four domains of experience; body & breath, feeling & sensation, mind states, and phenomena.

Eaarth: This spelling of the Earth is taken from Bill McKibben's book Eaarth. McKibben, a contemporary climate activist and founder of 350.

org, uses this spelling to represent the new geological earth reality we are moving into due to climate change.

It's like a great regal tree: This is a paragraph is from the ninth vow of Samantabhadra Bodhisattva from Chaper 40 of the Avatamsaka Sutra, a classical Mahayana Buddhist text.

The Ninth Vow: "I will accord with and take care of all these many kinds of beings, providing all manner of services and offerings for them. I will treat them with the same respect I show my own parents, teachers, elders, Arhats, and the Buddhas. I will serve them equally without difference. I will be a good physician for the sick and suffering. I will lead those who have lost their way to the right road. I will be a bright light for those in the dark night, and cause the poor and destitute to uncover hidden treasures. The Bodhisattva impartially benefits all living beings in this manner. Why is this? If a Bodhisattva accords with living beings, then she accords with and makes offerings to all Buddhas. If she can honor and serve living beings, then she honors and serves the Buddhas. If she makes living beings happy, she is making all Buddhas happy. Why is this? It is because all Buddhas take the mind of Great Compassion as their substance. Because of living beings, they develop Great Compassion. From Great Compassion the Bodhi Mind is born; and because of the Bodhi Mind they accomplish Supreme, Perfect Enlightenment."

"It is like a great regal tree growing in the rocks and sand of a barren wilderness. When the roots get water, the branches, leaves flowers, and fruits will all flourish. The Regal Bodhi-Tree growing in the wilderness of Birth and Death is the same. All living beings are its roots; all Buddhas and Bodhisattvas are its flowers and fruits. By benefiting all beings with the water of Great Compassion, one can realize the flowers and fruits of the bodhisattvas' and Buddhas' wisdom. Why is this? It is because by benefiting living beings with the water of Great Compassion, the Bodhisattvas attain Supreme, Perfect Enlightenment. Therefore, Bodhi belongs to living beings. Without living beings, no Bodhisattva could achieve Supreme, Perfect Enlightenment. Good person, you should understand these principles in this way: When the mind is impartial towards all living beings, one can accomplish full and perfect Great

Compassion. By using the mind of Great Compassion to accord with living beings, one perfects the offering of the Dharma to the Buddhas. In this way the bodhisattva constantly accords with living beings. Even when the realms of empty space are exhausted, the realms of living beings are exhausted, the karmas of living beings are exhausted, and the afflictions of living beings are exhausted, I will still accord endlessly, continuously, in thought after thought, without cease. My body, speech and mind never weary of these deeds."

Acknowledgements

To the First People of the /Xam. To the /Xam narrators and their transcribers-translators. To the linguists of the late 1800's, Bleek and Lloyd, who captured a dying language and made accessible the stories, poems, songs and narratives of the Khoisan. To Alan James for inspiration and use of translations from his book "The First Bushmen's Path, stories, songs and testimonies of the /Xam of the northern Cape." To the University of KwaZulu Natal Press for permission to reprint the poems and lines used from Alan James's book.

To Kittisaro, my beloved husband and Dharma partner, who has illuminated my understanding of the Dharma in so many ways, and who awakened me to core insights within the Heart Sutra.

To Cathy Wickham for the perfect (awesome!) foreword to this poem. To Ian Rees for deepening my appreciation of the Heart Sutra. To the City of 10,000 Buddha's and John Peacock for their translations of the Heart Sutra which influenced the translation used in this book. To Martin Randall, for a hint, leading me to the power of Dis Al. To Joanne Fedler whose get-down wondrous writing retreat inspired me on! To Lynette Denny for heartfelt encouragement and insightful feedback. To Andrew Harvey for his great inspiration and the line "a tsunami of black karma" which he said regards the appalling abuse of the animal kingdom through factory farming. And to Andrew Harvey for the phrase "the storm is coming" from indigenous people of the Amazon. Dismayed by government apathy at the Copenhagen Climate talks (2009) they took the stage and screamed sounds of animals being destroyed as the rain forest is clear cut; saying, "prepare yourselves, because the storm is coming." To Rumi for some lines from "This being human is a guest house," and Lao Tzu for his essential words on the Tao. To the people of South Africa who have overcome much. And to the Earth at the time of her crucifixion.

For information about Thanissara's teaching schedule: www.dharmagiri.org

Made in the USA
Charleston, SC
28 January 2014